JAPANESE AMERICAN CONFINEMENT CAMPS

by Clara MacCarald

FOCUS
READERS

www.focusreaders.com

Focus Readers is distributed by North Star Editions:
sales@northstareditions.com | 888-417-0195

Produced for Focus Readers by Red Line Editorial.

Content Consultant: Allan W. Austin, Professor of History & Government, Misericordia University

Photographs ©: AP Images, cover, 1, 25, 14–15, 38; US Navy/AP Images, 4–5; Red Line Editorial, 7, 31; Francis Stewart/National Archives and Records Administration, 8–9, 19, 33; Dorothea Lange/National Archives and Records Administration, 11, 17; National Archives and Records Administration, 13, 21, 28–29, 35; Ansel Adams/Manzanar War Relocation Center photographs/Library of Congress, 22–23; Masayuki/Shutterstock Images, 27; Joe McCelleand/National Archives and Records Administration, 36–37; Casey Page/The Billings Gazette/AP Images, 41; Hikaru Iwaski/National Archives and Records Administration, 42–43; Yone Kudo/National Archives and Records Administration, 44

ISBN
978-1-63517-875-3 (hardcover)
978-1-63517-976-7 (paperback)
978-1-64185-179-4 (ebook pdf)
978-1-64185-078-0 (hosted ebook)

Library of Congress Control Number: 2018931681

Printed in the United States of America
Mankato, MN
May, 2018

ABOUT THE AUTHOR

Clara MacCarald is a freelance writer with a master's degree in biology. She lives with her family in an off-grid house nestled in the forests of central New York. When not parenting her daughter, she spends her time writing nonfiction books for kids.

TABLE OF CONTENTS

CHAPTER 1

MISTAKEN FOR THE ENEMY

On December 7, 1941, Japanese planes bombed Pearl Harbor in Hawaii. Japan was in the middle of fighting World War II (1939–1945). Japanese leaders thought the United States would soon enter the war. They hoped a surprise attack would give Japan an advantage.

In 1941, thousands of Japanese Americans lived in the United States. Immigrants born in Japan, or the **Issei**, could not become US citizens.

Smoke rises from destroyed battleships after the attack on Pearl Harbor.

But most of the Issei's children, called the **Nisei**, were born on US soil. This made them US citizens.

After the attack, many people in the United States accused Japanese Americans of siding with Japan. In February 1942, US President Franklin D. Roosevelt signed Executive Order 9066. This order allowed the US military to move Japanese Americans who were living on the West Coast. Any Japanese American in the **exclusionary area** would be forced to move to prison-like camps. The government called them *internment* camps.

Internment is a process in which a country at war arrests and imprisons noncitizen enemies. However, the 120,000 Japanese Americans forcibly removed from the West Coast were not arrested. In this case, the term *internment* is incorrect. Instead, many historians use terms such as *incarceration* or *confinement*. These terms better reflect the unjust nature of the camps.

Japanese Americans forced into confinement had only a few days to prepare. They left behind homes, schools, and businesses. Half of them were children, and two-thirds were US citizens. Even so, their country treated them as enemies.

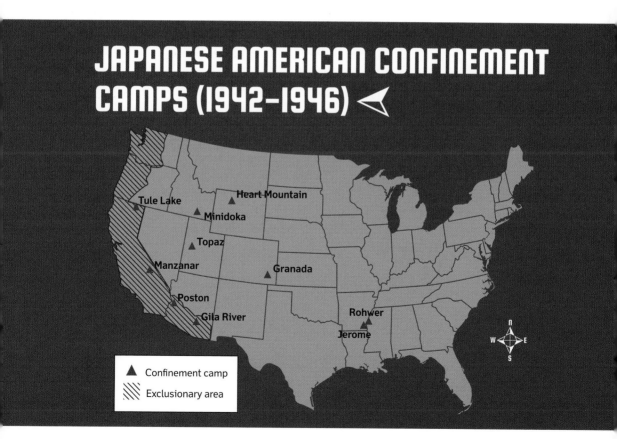

JAPANESE AMERICAN CONFINEMENT CAMPS (1942–1946) ◁

Tule Lake

Heart Mountain

Minidoka

Topaz

Manzanar

Granada

Poston

Gila River

Rohwer

Jerome

N
W ✦ E
S

▲ Confinement camp

╲╲╲ Exclusionary area

CHAPTER 2

AN ADVENTURE GONE WRONG

Before the attack on Pearl Harbor, 10-year-old Sato Hashizume loved school. But afterward, other children began to harass her for being Japanese American. To avoid being bullied, Sato pretended to be from China, a US **ally**. When Sato learned that her family would be moving to a confinement camp, she was excited. She thought it would be an adventure.

Japanese Americans' luggage is sorted after arrival at the Minidoka confinement camp.

Sato was 10 years old when the government sent her family to a detention center in Portland, Oregon. Detention centers housed Japanese Americans until confinement camps were ready. The center wasn't what Sato had expected. Barbed wire surrounded the grounds, and armed guards patrolled the fence. The bathrooms and showers had no stalls. The apartments in the **barracks** weren't built for privacy, either. Families shared one tiny room, and the walls of the rooms didn't reach the ceiling.

Because the land had been used for livestock, the smell of manure wafted through the wood floors. The **mess hall** was even worse. Families ate their meals among flies. Sato noticed that the food was slimy and strangely colored. It was nothing like the rice and fresh vegetables she ate at home. Many of the dishes were poorly washed.

Families at the confinement camp in Manzanar, California, eat a meal in the mess hall.

As a result, food poisoning was a common problem in the detention center.

Sometimes, Sato and her friends would go to the fence and make faces at the guards. The children's parents told them the fence was dangerous. At one point, a guard killed a Japanese American man who was trying to leave the center. After that, the children listened to their parents.

When summer ended, Sato's family was sent to the Minidoka confinement camp in Idaho. Sato and her sister kept up their spirits by singing songs on the train. Once they arrived, her family was crammed into a small room heated with coal.

In December 1944, the US Supreme Court ruled that the government could not confine loyal citizens. In anticipation of the ruling, Roosevelt decided to end the confinement of all Japanese Americans. Although the war wasn't over, the confinement camps would slowly be closed, and Japanese Americans could return home. Sato's father found an apartment and job in Salt Lake City, Utah. Sato had never been to Utah. By now, she had learned to be wary of new adventures.

Sato found the wide streets of Salt Lake City to be strange and lonely. In addition, her father made very little money at his new job. When he

The library at the Minidoka confinement camp collected resources to help families plan their departures.

slipped and hurt himself, he wasn't able to work anymore. Sato had to find a job. She cleaned and cooked for a white family before and after school.

After a year, Sato's family returned to Portland. At school, non–Japanese American students ignored Sato. The principal even warned two Nisei kids not to cause trouble. It took many years before Sato talked about her experience in the camps, even with other Japanese Americans.

CHAPTER 3

FRIENDS AND FAMILY

William J. Akiyoshi was born a US citizen in Eatonville, Washington, in 1928. He grew up in a close-knit Japanese American community. Many Issei had moved to Eatonville for jobs in the logging industry. Nisei kids in Eatonville attended school and played sports such as basketball and baseball. After the school day was over, they attended Japanese language school. There, they learned about Japanese culture and language.

Japanese Americans off the coast of Washington took ferries while going to detention centers.

In May 1942, everything changed for the Japanese American community in Eatonville. All residents of Japanese ancestry were forced to move to the Puyallup detention center a few miles north of town. At age 14, William had to say goodbye to his school, his home, and the only town he ever knew.

The US Army had hurriedly built the center on the racetrack of the Western Washington Fairgrounds. When William's family arrived, they trudged through the gates and to the barracks. A tiny room awaited them. Everyone had to share a bathroom and a cold shower. They didn't know how long they would be living in the cramped quarters.

William had new responsibilities at the camp. He helped care for his siblings, including a baby brother who was born at the camp. He also

Children in the confinement camps passed time by reading, going to school, and playing games.

washed his own laundry. This was a challenge because of the center's cold water.

After four months at Puyallup, William's family was forced to move to a camp in Idaho. Families left early in the morning on moving day. For William, the train ride was a welcome change from the center. Unfortunately, the Minidoka camp awaited him at the end of the trip.

Dusty, empty land surrounded the camp. Inside, the army had started building schools and stores. But the work wasn't finished until after people moved in. William's family lived in a room without much furniture. The camp also had a recreation hall where William and his friends played games. Still, the camp felt like a prison. Armed guards watched the camp from tall towers.

Soon after the camps were created, some Japanese Americans were allowed to leave confinement. US politicians worried that Japanese Americans would grow dependent on the government. So, they allowed some Japanese

➤ THINK ABOUT IT

Many of the confinement camps were built in remote, desolate areas. Why do you think the US Army chose these locations instead of towns and cities?

▲ A train carries 600 Japanese Americans from the Puyallup detention center to the Minidoka confinement camp.

Americans to leave the camps to attend college or work jobs. However, with the exclusionary area still in place, Japanese Americans were not allowed on the West Coast.

To leave the camps, Japanese Americans needed to move away from the West Coast. They also needed a person willing to support them in their new community. After a year and a half in confinement, William's family joined relatives in Denver, Colorado. For William, time in the camps was over.

JIM AKAGI

At the time of the attack on Pearl Harbor, Jim Akagi was a fifth grader in Seattle, Washington. Later, Jim wrote about his experience: "I felt so embarrassed because I was practically the only Japanese around the district. The rest were all Americans. I did not go out so much as I used to on account of being Japanese."

Like other Japanese American families, Jim's family was sent to the Puyallup detention center. After that, they made the move to the Minidoka camp in Idaho. The new camp was horribly dusty. But according to Jim, the winter brought a little fun: "A lake by our place froze, so I went ice-skating again, which reminded me about Seattle very much." Unfortunately, the similarities to Jim's old home stopped there. The climate in Minidoka was more extreme than in Seattle. Temperatures could be as high as 115 degrees

The Minidoka confinement camp collected Christmas gifts donated by people across the United States.

Fahrenheit (46°C) and as low as –30 degrees Fahrenheit (–34°C).

When the holiday season came, it was hard for Jim to get excited. Still, the adults in the camp tried to bring the kids some Christmas cheer. Jim wrote all about his gifts: "I got a scarf, color pencils, and a knife for Christmas from Santa Claus." He tried to keep his spirits up.

Jim Akagi. "My First Experience in a War." *Special Collections.* University of Washington Libraries, n.d. Web. 8 Mar. 2018.

CHAPTER 4

KEEPING BUSY

Setsuko Izumi was born in Los Angeles, California, in 1932. Growing up, Setsuko had a very busy schedule. Like many Nisei, she attended English school, Japanese school, and **Sunday school**. Her mother also insisted she take piano lessons. In her free time, Setsuko played with her friends. Some of Setsuko's friends were Japanese Americans, and some were white.

Japanese American girls play volleyball at the Manzanar confinement camp.

They jumped rope and played with dolls. Some days, Setsuko joined her father fishing.

Setsuko's normal life came to a halt when she was 10 years old. After the attack on Pearl Harbor, her family was sent to Santa Anita, a detention center in California. When they arrived, they found out that the center had previously been a racetrack. It smelled of horses. Dust was everywhere. Setsuko attended school in a large hall, which made it difficult to hear lessons.

One day, guards instructed Setsuko's family to board a train. After a long trip, the train rolled into

> **THINK ABOUT IT**

Families moving to confinement camps could take only two suitcases per person. If you were forced to leave your home with two suitcases, what would you pack?

▲ Japanese Americans in Los Angeles, California, board cars and buses as they leave for confinement.

a swampy part of Arkansas. The passengers had arrived at the Rohwer confinement camp.

Arkansas was very different from Los Angeles. In the winter, Setsuko was amazed by snow. Snow had fallen in Los Angeles the year she was born, but she'd never seen it herself. The rest of her time in Rohwer wasn't as exciting. People had to walk on boards to avoid slipping in mud. Mosquitoes bred in the puddles and spread disease.

Setsuko couldn't leave the camp or improve its conditions, but she could keep busy. School was one way to pass the time. But Setsuko's new school was roughly put together. Desks had been made from coarse logs. Outside of school, Setsuko played kick the can and other games with her friends. She also joined a Girl Scout troop.

People in the camp continued to celebrate Japanese culture. Setsuko learned to play the koto, a Japanese string instrument. Setsuko's birthday, March 3, fell on a Japanese holiday called Girls' Day. On Girls' Day, girls display beautifully dressed dolls in their homes. At the camp, people brought their dolls to the mess hall. Setsuko celebrated her special day by looking at all the dolls.

When families first arrived at the camp, guards watched them carefully. But over the years,

▲ The Japanese doll festival held on Girls' Day is called *Hinamatsuri*.

monitoring decreased. One day, Setsuko and her friends were able to sneak under the barbed wire without being seen. One friend carried a jug. After a short walk, they found a local store. They bought soda and poured it into their jug to bring to the camp. They were scared sneaking back, but they were also excited to have gotten out. Setsuko didn't leave the camp for good until after the war.

CHAPTER 5

A QUESTION OF LOYALTY

Ben Takeshita was born a US citizen in California in 1930. After the attack on Pearl Harbor, Ben felt pressured to prove his loyalty to the United States. His two older brothers had lived in Japan for several years. When the Japanese government tried to recruit them for the Japanese army, they both refused. At home, Ben saved coins to buy **defense stamps**, which would help fund the US war effort.

Approximately 33,000 Japanese Americans served in the US military during World War II.

Neither Ben's actions nor his brothers' made a difference. Ben was 11 years old when the US government forced his family to leave their home. His mother told the children to wear extra layers of clothing so they could carry more things in their suitcases. Still, Ben had to leave his toys and baseball bat. At the detention center, his family created beds by filling canvas bags with hay.

On a particularly hot day, Ben's family was forced to move to a desert camp in Topaz, Utah. Wind blew dust into their faces as they arrived at the camp. It wasn't long before Ben learned the dangers of the camp. One day, guards shot an older man who was gathering seashells too close to the fence. Ben and his friends learned to be careful.

In 1943, adults in the camp received a government-issued loyalty questionnaire. One question asked whether the person was willing to swear loyalty to the United States. Another asked whether the person was willing to fight in the US Army or otherwise support the war. These were tough questions. Answering yes could cause the Issei to lose their Japanese citizenship.

LOYALTY QUESTION #28 ◄

"Will you swear unqualified allegiance to the United States of America and faithfully defend the United States from any or all attack by foreign or domestic forces, and forswear any form of allegiance or obedience to the Japanese emperor, or any other foreign government, power, or organization?"

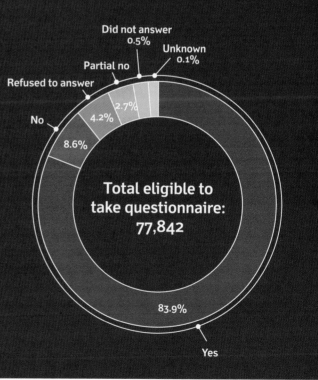

Did not answer 0.5%

Unknown 0.1%

Partial no

Refused to answer

2.7%

No

4.2%

8.6%

Total eligible to take questionnaire: 77,842

83.9%

Yes

Because they couldn't become US citizens, they might have no legal country. Nisei worried that answering yes would lead them to be **drafted**.

Ben's brother felt insulted by the questionnaire and answered no to both loyalty questions. Ben's parents didn't want their family to be separated, so they also answered no. Because of this, the army assumed Ben's family was disloyal. The army moved them and others who answered "no-no" to Tule Lake in California. People at the Tule Lake camp thought they might be sent to Japan.

When food became scarce at Tule Lake, families grew angry. Some of their anger erupted into

> **THINK ABOUT IT**
>
> Why do you think some loyal US citizens answered no to the loyalty questions?

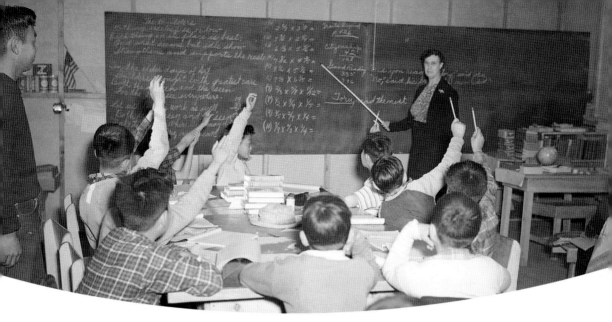

Students attend grammar school at the Tule Lake confinement camp.

violence. At one point, guards killed an unarmed Japanese American man. Later, soldiers took Ben's brother away. Ben didn't know where they had taken him or whether his brother would be killed.

Ben's brother came back months later. He had been questioned and threatened by US soldiers. In 1945, Ben was finally allowed to return home with his family. But his brother didn't want to stay in the United States after the treatment he'd received. He moved to Japan.

EDNA HIRABAYASHI

Edna Hirabayashi was born in 1928 in Seattle. When war broke out between her home country and her ancestors' country, it broke her heart. Later on, she wrote about the days following the attack. "Five days later, my father was taken into custody by the immigration authorities as a dangerous alien," she wrote. "Wasn't he trusted after he had lived here for so long?"

In April 1942, Edna's family was sent to the Puyallup detention center. Edna teared up as they left Seattle. She had lived there for 14 years—her whole life. Fortunately, there were some moments at the camp that cheered her up. Edna wrote: "Our American friends came to visit us in the visiting room of the camp." The visit brought Edna a little piece of home.

Next, Edna's family was sent to the Minidoka camp in Idaho. Leaving her home state made Edna

A view of the mess hall, sanitization building, and barracks at the Minidoka confinement camp

very sad. "On our arrival here, we were greeted by clouds of dust blowing into our faces, and people giving us muffled 'Hellos' because they held handkerchieves over their noses," she wrote.

Edna tried to make the best of her situation, but staying positive wasn't always easy. Mostly, she looked ahead: "With all my heart I wish to forget these incidents, hoping they will be mended in some way in the future."

Edna Hirabayashi. "A Review." *Special Collections*. University of Washington Libraries, n.d. Web. 8 Mar. 2018.

CHAPTER 6

SCOUTING AT CAMP

Norman Mineta was born a US citizen in 1931 and grew up in San Jose, California. He loved playing baseball and belonging to a Boy Scout troop. Japanese American communities saw **scouting** as a very American activity. They also admired the values taught in scouting, such as loyalty and good citizenship.

After the attack on Pearl Harbor, Norman's family was sent to Heart Mountain in Wyoming.

Japanese Americans at the Granada confinement camp created a Boy Scout headquarters.

▲ Many of the confinement camps, such as this one in Manzanar, were built in a rush.

Norman was 10 years old at the time. On the day of the trip, Norman dressed in his scouting uniform. His display of American loyalty did not make a difference. Officials still saw Norman as an enemy of the United States. They took away his baseball bat, saying it could be used as a weapon.

After an initial stay at a detention center, Norman's family took a long train ride to the middle of nowhere. Dry land, dotted with short and shrubby plants, stretched in every direction. Harsh winds blew up dust.

Inside the Heart Mountain camp, Norman found hastily constructed buildings. The walls of his family's room were made of paper and tar. To keep the room warm, Norman fetched coal from a big bin in the freezing yard. At night, he had to take a long, cold walk to the bathroom. No school had been built yet for the camp. To give the kids something to do, parents created scout troops.

Scouting at the camp wasn't easy. The scouts had to find their own equipment. They couldn't hike far inside the camp, and they couldn't take swimming tests, either. Eventually, the scouts used hand tools to dig out a swimming pool.

Fortunately, a nearby stream provided a site for overnight camping.

Parents at the camp decided to hold a Boy Scout jamboree. Because Japanese Americans weren't allowed to leave, they invited scouts from outside the camp to come inside and join them. Only one troop accepted their invitation.

Norman hadn't seen many white kids since leaving his home. He and a white boy named Alan Simpson set up a tent together. Alan convinced Norman to help him play a prank on a bully. Together, the two flooded the boy's tent with water. Norman and Alan became lifelong friends.

In 1943, the government allowed Norman's family to leave the camp. Norman's father had found a job in Chicago, Illinois. Though Norman had escaped the camp, he couldn't forget his experience. At a restaurant, he tried to clean up

In 2011, Mineta and Simpson visited a new museum at the long-closed Heart Mountain confinement camp.

his table as if he were still in the mess hall. Then he remembered he was finally free.

Norman went on to be president of his high school's student body. In 1974, he was elected to a higher office: the US House of Representatives. Norman would play an important role in pushing the US government to make **amends** for its treatment of Japanese Americans.

CHAPTER 7

THE END OF THE CAMPS

When Executive Order 9066 was announced, some Japanese Americans resisted. The cases of four Nisei even reached the Supreme Court. In 1944, the Nisei's resistance led to Roosevelt's Public Proclamation 21, which would slowly put an end to the camps. As World War II continued, some camps began to close. And in January 1945, the government started allowing Japanese Americans to return to the West Coast.

Some Japanese American children leaving confinement had never lived outside the camps.

Japanese Americans at the Heart Mountain confinement camp say their goodbyes as they leave the camp.

Few Japanese Americans could return to their old lives. Homes had been lost or damaged. Some towns posted signs saying Japanese Americans were not welcome. Many Japanese Americans moved to new parts of the country.

On September 2, 1945, Japan surrendered to the United States and its wartime allies. More than six months later, the last confinement camp closed. After the war, the attitudes of other

Americans toward Japanese Americans slowly changed. Nisei units in the US military had won many honors during the war. Japan even became a US ally. Finally, in 1952, the US government passed a law allowing Japanese immigrants to become US citizens.

Many Japanese Americans pushed for the US government to apologize for its past actions. The government had taken away Japanese Americans' rights and uprooted their lives. In 1988, the government issued an official apology. It also made a $20,000 payment to every living survivor of the camps. However, no amount of money could make up for what survivors had lost. Today, their memories of the camps serve as a reminder of the injustices against Japanese Americans. By remembering the past, Americans can work to prevent similar injustices from happening again.

CHILDREN IN JAPANESE AMERICAN CONFINEMENT CAMPS

Write your answers on a separate piece of paper.

1. Write a paragraph that summarizes Chapter 1.

2. Rather than resisting, most Japanese Americans followed government orders to move to the camps. Do you think they were right to do so? Why or why not?

3. In which year did Franklin D. Roosevelt order the forced removal of Japanese Americans on the West Coast?

    A. 1941
    B. 1942
    C. 1945

4. Why couldn't William Akiyoshi's family return home when they left the Minidoka confinement camp?

    A. The exclusionary area was still in effect.
    B. They had answered no to the loyalty questions.
    C. They were forced to move to Colorado.

Answer key on page 48.

GLOSSARY

ally
A nation that helps another nation in a war.

amends
Something done or given to make up for a wrongdoing.

barracks
Buildings designed to house soldiers or large groups of people.

defense stamps
Stamps that US citizens bought from the government to help fund World War II.

drafted
Required by the government to serve in the military.

exclusionary area
The area on the US West Coast from which Japanese Americans were forcibly removed during World War II.

Issei
Immigrants from Japan.

mess hall
A gathering place where soldiers or other groups of people eat.

Nisei
Children of immigrants from Japan.

scouting
The activities associated with scout troops, such as camping, hiking, and helping others.

Sunday school
Classes that children take on Sundays to learn about Christianity.

TO LEARN MORE

BOOKS

Atkins, Laura, and Stan Yogi. *Fred Korematsu Speaks Up.* Berkeley, CA: Heyday, 2017.

Marrin, Albert. *Uprooted: The Japanese American Experience during World War II.* New York: Alfred A. Knopf, 2016.

Otfinoski, Steven. *World War II.* New York: Scholastic, 2017.

NOTE TO EDUCATORS

Visit **www.focusreaders.com** to find lesson plans, activities, links, and other resources related to this title.

INDEX

Answer Key: 1. Answers will vary; **2.** Answers will vary; **3.** B; **4.** A